HERBS FOR WITCHCRAFT

The Green Witches' Grimoire of Plant Magick

By Didi Clarke

Disclaimer:
While I have performed all these spells myself, your results may vary.

*If you'd like to be notified when I publish a new book or have something exciting in the works, be sure to sign up for my mailing list. You'll receive a **FREE** color magick correspondence chart when you do! Follow this link to subscribe:*

https://mailchi.mp/01863952b9ff/didi-clarke-mailing-list

CONTENTS

CHAPTER 1: WELCOME TO THE WORLD OF PLANT MAGICK

The natural world is the source of all life for humans. It keeps us fed, it gives us the resources we need to build and maintain a society, and its beauty provides us with emotional nourishment as well. However, to witches, nature is much more than this. It is a symbol and source of spiritual life and Divine power.

Herbs and witchcraft go hand in hand. When you think of stereotypical depictions of a witch, what do you imagine? Do you see a green-skinned old woman gently stirring some herbal concoction in a cauldron? While that's not the most flattering portrayal of us, it does get one thing right—our use of items from the earth in magick!

While we use herbs and other plants quite frequently to work our will, the natural world is not simply a tool at a witch's disposal. It is sacred and deserving of honor— we don't just turn to it for help, we also celebrate and respect it!

In *Herbs for Witchcraft*, it's my goal to introduce you to both of these aspects of green witchcraft. I'll show you the techniques necessary for studying and harnessing the power of plants, but I also want to take some time to explore the philosophy of nature that structures this practice. Learning one without the other will leave you seriously lacking in the herbal magick department!

What is Green Witchcraft?

Before we go any further, I want to take a moment to define a word I just used that might be unfamiliar to some readers: green witchcraft.

This word most commonly refers to witches who work with nature-based items and deities. This includes most Wiccans, but being Wiccan is by no means a requirement for being a green witch—most of the belief systems associated with Paganism or European folk religions have aspects to them that could be considered "green" in a spiritual sense.

At the end of the day, if you have a desire to explore the magickal properties of plants, become closer to nature, and learn how to live in harmony with it, you can safely call yourself a green witch. For a deeper exploration of the beliefs of green witchcraft, take a look at chapter two in this book, where I outline some of the major tenets.

What You'll Find in This Book

This book serves as an overview of all things related to plant magick. From learning what herbs are best for certain purposes to planning spells based on the season, *Herbs for Witchcraft* takes you through everything you need to get started in the world of green witchcraft.

In particular, we'll look at the following things:

- Beliefs of green witchcraft
- Nature-based Gods and Goddesses
- Communicating with the natural world
- Plant-based spells and rituals
- Plant folklore
- And much more!

Mother Nature awaits! Are you ready to take this journey with her?

Then let's begin!

CHAPTER 2: WHAT DOES A GREEN WITCH BELIEVE?

Plant and herbal magick are largely about working spells with resources from the natural world. However, green witchcraft is actually a bit more complex than simply deciding what tools to use. In many ways, it is a complete way of life that involves not only magick but how we view our relationship to the natural world as well.

In this chapter, I'm going to look at some of the basic tenets of green magick that make it unique within the world of witchcraft practices. If you've got an interest in plant magick, many of these beliefs will probably already sound familiar to you. But it's incredibly important to emphasize them at the beginning, because they will affect the potency of your spellwork.

Think of it this way—you wouldn't invoke a god or goddess from a place of ignorance or disrespect, would you? Of course not! And those that do are likely to find their particular deity isn't particularly receptive to their petitions. Similarly, the natural world has the power to lend a hand (or withhold help) to witches as it sees fit. Approaching it with the utmost understanding and respect is just as important as approaching a God in the same way.

The following list of beliefs or attitudes attributed to green witchcraft are by no means exhaustive. Largely, they come from my own understanding of and work within the natural world. However, they will provide you a nice starting point to begin your journey and deepen your appreciation of Mother Nature and all her gifts.

Nature is sacred.

If you polled a large group of Wiccans or witches, chances are, most would agree with the statement, "Nature is sacred." However, it's particularly important within the world of green witchcraft.

Nature isn't simply a collection of trees, plants, herbs, flowers, and other wildlife. It is a physical manifestation of the Divine. When you find yourself marveling at the beauty of a dense forest or gently rolling hills full of green grass and wildflowers, you are having a direct encounter with the Divine spirit of the planet.

I'm by no means anti-science, and in the strictest sense, the natural world is indeed a collection of atoms and molecules and cells. However, it goes so much deeper than that. Nature is a mystery and a miracle. It's wise beyond human understanding, and it nourishes us physically and spiritually. Nature shows us the best of what this universe has to offer, and it weaves its power in us from birth through life to death. What else could you call something like that besides sacred?

Humans are not the masters of nature.

Despite modern man's best efforts, humans will never be the masters of nature. At best, we can only proudly say that we are a part of it. When we practice plant magick, it's important that we remember this and stay humble.

While witchcraft may in some part be about exerting our will upon the world, that's not the whole story. The only reason we can hope to accomplish that is because the natural world allows it. Treating nature as an equal, not a servant, is the only path a green witch can morally take. And it's the only one that will yield practical results.

Cultivating a sense of gratitude toward nature will improve your magickal practice and may benefit your life in other ways as well. Cultivating an attitude of arrogance and dominion over the natural world is basically just begging for karmic retribution from—you guessed it—the natural world.

Green witches must protect nature.

We may not be the masters of nature, but humans are definitely experts at destroying it in new and terrifying ways. To follow the path of the green witch, you must be willing to do what you can to prevent this.

Primarily, this means thinking about the impact that your own life and magickal practice have on the earth. It means not being wasteful with the natural materials you use. It means thinking about your carbon footprint and opting for home-grown plants and herbs instead of those that require wasteful packaging and shipping (when possible). It means thinking beyond your own life and finding ways to preserve the natural world for generations to come.

We all have our part to play in protecting nature, and one of the most important tasks a green witch has is finding her own unique role in this exciting and necessary work.

Nature is not all sunshine and roses.

From natural disasters to good old poison ivy, it should be clear that nature is not always our friend. However, for those of us who have such a deep love for the natural world, it can be easy to take on the mindset that it's possible to live in perfect bliss and harmony with Mother Nature. But trust me, this is definitely not the case.

A good green witch has a healthy respect for both the amazing and terrible things that the natural world is capable of. This attitude shouldn't devolve into a fear of nature, but we've got to use common sense.

This really should go without saying, but when working with natural materials, keep track of what's poisonous and what's not. Keep track of what you're personally allergic to. Don't put yourself in harm's way to find rare and exotic plants. Just because you're working magick doesn't mean you're exempt from the laws of nature.

On a more philosophical level, this means realizing that nature can be fickle and dangerous. And it means understanding that a better relationship with nature won't solve all of your problems—which, more often than not, have very human origins.

The natural world can benefit the life of a green witch in amazing and unexpected ways, but never forget that Mother Nature can (and will) bare her teeth from time to time.

Nature is a learning experience.

If there's one thing I want you to take away from the chapter, it's this—understanding and exploring the natural world is a learning process. No one is a perfect green witch right out of the gate. Having the right mindset when working magickally with plants is important, but ultimately, there's no checklist of beliefs that will perfectly guide you all the time.

But I've found that if you trust your intuition, your good intentions, and the wisdom of the natural world, the path of the green witch can be the journey of a lifetime.

CHAPTER 3: NATURE-BASED MEDITATION

When was the last time you took some time to really focus on nature? For most of us, it's difficult to spend an extended period of time focusing on anything! And when we do, it usually has to do with the responsibilities of everyday life—focusing on your job, focusing on your family, etc.

However, to really tap into the power and wonder of plant magick, you need to be willing to dedicate some time to ponder and contemplate your subject matter—the natural world. So, in this chapter, I'm going to show you a few nature-based meditation techniques for centering your thoughts and focusing your intentions.

When I have the time, I like to preface my spellwork with one of these meditations. They're a great way to really bring you into the mindset of a green witch. That being said, even if you can't regularly fit a meditation session into your schedule on top of magick as well, I would recommend trying these out from time to time as a way to refresh and recharge. I think you'll find that they can be just as inspiring and empowering as ritual work itself!

Sensory Meditation

Despite the stereotype, meditation doesn't have to be about closing your eyes and emptying your mind of all thoughts. In fact, this meditation technique is all about contemplation of the natural world. It's meant to put you in touch with nature on a deeper level and help you appreciate both the complexity and simplicity of the world we inhabit.

To begin, find a place outdoors where you can be free from distractions. I like to find a nice place to sit on the ground, but if that won't work for you, sitting in a chair or standing up are fine too. Being comfortable is important for this—you want to be able to focus all your attention on your natural surroundings.

When you've found your spot, simply begin observing. Don't try to think too much about this—allow your focus to travel where it may.

What's the first thing your eye is drawn to in this setting? Spend some time really taking that object in. Your focus doesn't have to be too demanding or intense, but allow yourself to study it to the point that you could realistically recreate it in your mind's eye.

As you continue to study, allow your focus to gradually widen to include more than just that first object. Notice how it fits into its larger surroundings.

Does it stand out like a bright flower in a field or does it meld into a larger whole like the individual blades of grass in that same field? Keep broadening your scope of focus until the things you see no longer feel like isolated objects but interlocking parts of the natural world.

Slowly, begin to incorporate more of your senses into the process. Can you hear the gentle rush of wind? Do you feel the dew on the grass? Can you smell the fragrant perfume of a fresh blossom? Allow this new sensory data to create an even more vivid picture within your mind.

Keep in mind, this particular meditation isn't about having an "a-ha!" moment. It has no goal beyond becoming keenly aware of your surroundings. This can feel frustrating at first, but as you allow your focus to both expand and deepen, you'll discover the pleasure of simply sitting and observing. You've got a front-row seat to the magickal symphony that is our earth!

Continue with this meditation as long as your attention will allow it. After you've taken a big-picture view of your surroundings, try your hand at doing the opposite—focusing intently on all the minute details of one small thing.

Notice the cracks and ridges in the tree bark. Trace the curvature of a single flower petal. Discover the ant journeying up a blade of grass. You'll soon find that there are surprising and complex worlds within the small space of a single object.

There's no required time limit with sensory meditation, but I find that I need at least 20 to 30 minutes to really get into the groove of things. If this isn't doable for you, try starting with a smaller length of time and increasing it as your focus and observation skills improve. Over time, you'll find that simply "being" in the world is no longer a chore or task but rather a deeply uplifting, spiritual experience.

Touch Meditation

The other meditation I want to share with you is similar to the sensory meditation technique, but it's a bit more specific and can be performed outdoors or indoors. With it, you'll be focusing on a specific nature-based object.

The first step is to find your object, and I recommend choosing a plant or herb that you will be working into a ritual. This technique is all about getting a feel for a particular plant's energy, so it makes sense to choose something that you'll be working firsthand with.

As with the sensory meditation, begin by simply observing your object. You can place it on a table or hold it in your hands at first—the important thing is to take some time to be with the object. Follow its contours. View it from different angles. Set a detailed image of it deep within your mind.

If you're not already holding the object, now is the time to pick it up. Feel the sensations it creates on your fingers. Is it rough? Smooth? Does its texture change in different places?

Here's where things get witchy—what can you intuit about the plant's energy from how it feels? It may seem surprising, but plants and herbs hold spiritual value and mystery, and coming into physical contact with them can help reveal some of that to you. Does it have a gentle energy? A powerful energy?

It might feel silly at first, but take some time to really think about this. You'd be surprised by what you can learn from plants. In the next chapter, I'll show you some techniques that will take this particular intuitive practice even deeper, but just getting a feel for a plant's energy is a good start for now.

CHAPTER 4: COMMUNICATING WITH PLANTS

I t may seem a little ridiculous at first, but plants actually have a lot to tell us, and communication with them is possible. And for successful plant magick, it's almost a necessity.

Now, don't expect your azalea bushes to strike up a full-blown conversation with you anytime soon, but there's no denying that plants and herbs are full of spiritual wisdom that can be shared with us.

Developing Your Intuition

Largely, these messages come through intuition, which is a skill that every witch should work hard to develop, no matter your area of expertise. Intuition is a gift that operates on the level of spirit or energy—while something may appear perfectly normal from a physical standpoint, humans are pretty good feeling or intuiting that something is amiss.

From a plant magick perspective, one of the best things you can do to develop a more personal, communicative bond with plants is simply to practice with them. So, start by picking a plant—any one will do for our purposes. Now, without thinking about it too much, as you look at the plant, what is the first word that comes to mind?

Don't censor yourself or try to come up with what you think the "right" answer is. Simply let whatever comes to mind do so unimpeded. This is an important point— many times when we think that our intuition has failed us, it's actually our rational mind that has failed us because we've allowed it to interfere with this subconscious action.

As you gain some experience with this practice, begin to focus your intuition on a particular aspect of plants—their magickal uses. Correspondence tables are a useful tool, and I provide one of my own later in the book, but I've found that plants have the ability to surprise us in terms of what they are good for. If you see a geranium and it leaves you with the impression of psychic ability, go with your gut and use it in psychic rituals—no matter what any correspondence guide may say!

Oftentimes, these intuitive, mystical associations will enhance the power of your magick because they are personal and come from within.

However, don't let your intuition be the end of the story—if you have a nagging feeling that a particular plant is good for particular spell, try it out! There's no way to improve your abilities without rolling the dice and testing them out.

In the early days of your intuitive development, you may find that you have many more misses than hits, but that's okay. No one is an expert right away. Stay persistent and allow your conscious mind to take a backseat to your subconscious— with time and patience you'll eventually strike the right balance.

Communicating Respect to Your Plants

As with human communication, plant communication isn't a one-way street, it's a conversation. And since we'll be using lots of plants and natural materials to work our will, it's got to be a respectful conversation—the plants are helping you out, after all.

Interacting with plants respectfully begins with not taking them for granted. Offering up a little prayer of thanksgiving when you harvest herbs or before you begin a ritual is a good starting place. It doesn't have to be anything elaborate or fancy—just speak from the heart. Let them know that they are offering themselves to you and that you appreciate it deeply.

Additionally, leaving an offering for plants is sometimes a good idea. This is especially true if you have to disfigure a plant but not completely uproot it—cutting a tree branch for a wand is a good example of this.

While this practice is perfectly acceptable, you must leave something in return. Nourishing the tree with water is a start, but also consider leaving something of value too, like a polished stone or a food offering. However, the specifics are not as important as the intention, so don't be afraid to get creative with your offerings. Use your intuition to discover what might be most pleasing to the tree itself.

CHAPTER 5: PLANT FOLKLORE

Plant magick is a traditional practice that has its origins in folk magick. While plants and other natural objects are frequently incorporated into "higher" forms of ritual work, plant magick is a tradition founded in the garden and in the kitchen of everyday witches. Because of its origins, folklore plays a big role in plant and herbal magick.

This folklore sometimes takes the form of traditional wisdom regarding plants— things like natural cures. But there is also a rich history of nature- and plant-based beings that populate the forests and fields of this world.

In this chapter, I'm going to take a look at some of the unique folklore and mythology of the plant world. This is by no means a complete history, but it is good to know a little something about your origins!

Knock on Wood

This is one magickal tradition that has made its way into mainstream consciousness. We use the phrase "knock on wood" every day to indicate a desire for good luck or fortune. But within the context of the modern world, it does sound a little odd. That's because this particular phrase has its origins in the pagans of ancient Germany.

As with many ancient cultures, these pagans believed that spirits resided in nature—particularly in trees. Depending on the exact species of tree, these spirits were thought to be able to bestow different gifts and blessings upon humans. So, they were definitely thought of as a force for good and fortune. By "knocking on wood" (i.e. the trees), these people hoped to bring themselves to the attention of the spirits and gain their favor.

The Green Man

For those of you familiar with architecture, the Green Man might already be familiar—it's typically an ornate sculpture or other decoration on an outside wall depicting a man made of leaves and vines. Strangely enough, these very pagan-looking Green Men often appear on Christian churches, especially in Europe.

However, sightings of this mysterious foliage fellow have been documented around the world. It seems like multiple, distinct cultures across time and space have seen fit to personify the natural world with a human face.

For modern Wiccans, the Green Man is sometimes a representation of or variation on the Horned God—the primary personification of the masculine side of the Divine. However, more generally, he also represents ecological awareness and serves as a reminder that we humans are not distinct from nature but rather are intimately intertwined with it.

Bluebells of Ireland

The natural beauty of Ireland is undeniable, so it's no wonder that they have a very rich history of plant-based folklore in their culture. What's particularly interesting are the stories surrounding bluebells, a type of flower whose blooms look like bells and range in color from light blue to dark purple. According to tradition, you could lure fairies out of hiding by ringing the bluebell blooms.

However, it was also seen as extremely unlucky to gather them in a bouquet, and some said that fairies also used bluebells to enchant unsuspecting humans. These beliefs might have been developed because the bluebell blossom, while incredibly beautiful, is also incredibly toxic. Even if that's the case, I'm not taking any chances with mischievous fairies!

Man-Eating Trees

As strange as it sounds, man-eating plants have a long history in traditional folklore. Many cultures in the world have some myths or stories surrounding carnivorous plants capable of dining on you or me.

Although there are no documented cases, there's talk of a plant in Nicaragua known as the Devil's Snare. According to legend, this vine-based plant had a thirst for blood and is capable of attaching itself to an unsuspecting victim, thanks to the thousands of small, mouth-like openings that populate its body.

Dryads

The dryads were tree spirits or nymphs in ancient Greek mythology and were most commonly associated with oak trees and the Goddess Artemis, who was said to be their friend. Dryads, according to myth, were also notoriously shy, which meant that human glimpses of them were few and far between.

It was believed that if a tree was killed, its associated dryad would also perish, which is why the Gods frequently punished humans who damaged or destroyed trees.

St. John's Wort

This wildflower, sometimes used for medicinal purposes, has a long magickal history. For centuries, it was used as a means of warding off evil spirits and other bad energies. In fact, it was so associated with the spiritual and magickal worlds that it developed nicknames like "devil's scourge" and "witch's herb."

In addition to its banishing properties, the blooming of St. John's Wort was also seen as a sign of an upcoming marriage. Some aspiring brides even used the wildflower to help them choose a suitable husband!

Rowan Trees

All types of trees hold a special place in most nature-based belief systems, but for some, the rowan tree is seen as particularly important. This species is found plentifully in Europe, which is why many of its ancient societies developed a number of spiritual uses for the tree.

Like St. John's Wort, rowan branches were thought to ward off evil spirits from one's home. In fact, folklore-minded Christians would often place a rowan branch under their beds on the night of Good Friday for just that purpose. Beyond that, rowan wood was thought to prevent the dead from rising as well, which is why the tree was often used for casket making.

Rowan is also a common choice for witches when creating a wand. While all trees hold some sort of power, rowan is considered to be especially spiritual. A good witch respects the rowan tree for the power it offers her.

CHAPTER 6: PLANT CORRESPONDENCES

W ithin the world of magick, correspondences are attributes and associations that apply to specific objects or concepts. Take an everyday example— many people associate the color red with love.

Finding the right correspondence is important for a green witch. Choosing herbs and plants that complement your magickal rituals will increase their potency.

In this chapter, I'm going to show you my own personal list of plant correspondences. These have served me well, but as your experience with plant magick increases, I highly recommend branching out and trying some of your own. This is one place where the meditation and communication exercises from the last few chapters will serve you well.

If you have difficulty finding a particular item in this list, don't let it worry you too much. Strong correspondences enhance your magick, but ultimately, that magick originates from your intention. Substitutions are fine, if you can find a plant with similar correspondences.

Apple: They might not be the most exotic fruit, but they are a good one nonetheless. Apples represent abundance, generosity, and the bounty of the earth. Before growing season, bless your garden by sprinkling apple skins across the dirt.

Basil: This common herb is good for money spells and prosperity magick. Slip a leaf in your wallet or purse to help attract good fortune. Basil is also useful for burnt offerings.

Blackberry: Blackberries represent bravery and admiration. They also make a good offering when invoking a God or Goddess.

Cedar: There's something heavenly about the smell of a cedar tree. And for good reason too—it's closely associated with the Divine. Cedar is a smart choice if you're looking to communicate with deities or spirits. A ring of cedar chips or shavings is also known to consecrate and protect the space inside the circle.

Cardamom: This fragrant spice is good for rest and relaxation—both physically and emotionally. Use it when you're looking for peace of mind or struggling with anger.

Daffodil: These bright, beautiful flowers are the color of our sun, and as such, they represent vitality and prosperity. They're perfect for spells about achieving your goals or advancing in a career.

Dandelion: They may be considered weeds, but dandelions have important magickal qualities. They represent goodness, honesty, and virtue and can help signal good intentions when dealing with deities or other metaphysical beings.

Dogwood: Dogwood blossoms are closely associated with creativity and artistic ability. Dogwood petals can be used to bless objects of creativity, like musical instruments or canvases. A branch from a dogwood tree can be fashioned into a wand that's ideal for a drawing down the moon ritual.

Fennel: This bulbous plant and stringy herb are ideal for weather-related magic. An offering of fennel can bring much-needed rains or keep severe weather at bay.

Forget-Me-Not: Like the name implies, forget-me-nots are loosely associated with memory. They make a good flower for rituals to commemorate the dead, but they can also be used to help come to terms with difficult events in your past.

Ginger: Turn to ginger if you're looking for charm, articulation, and people skills. It can be incorporated into rituals, but you can also just give it a good chew before a big presentation or a first date.

Goldenrod: These flowers make a good addition to rituals about protection and guidance. Use goldenrod to get in touch with your guardian angel or spirit guide.

Green Onion: They might be pungent, but green onions are ideal for all things related to dreams. Whether you want to improve your dream interpretation skills, remember your dreams more clearly, or experience symbolic dreams, green onions are the way to go.

Honeysuckle: It's fragrant, tasty, and spiritually powerful. Honeysuckle should be incorporated into your spring equinox celebration because of its associations with vegetation, growth, and new life. Other uses of honeysuckle include initiation rites, holiday celebrations, and consecration rituals.

Lavender: This fragrant and beautiful flower is associated with psychic and spiritual wisdom. It is imbued with Divine knowledge and is perfect for sages, seers, and prophets.

Lily: White lilies are a sign of deep love and devotion. They make a welcome addition to handfasting rituals (Wiccan weddings), but they can also be used in love spells and potions. Lilies may also represent purification and innocence.

Mint: The herb with a kick, mint is a symbol of good luck and serendipity. Additionally, sleeping with a sprig under your pillow is thought to bring prophetic dreams.

Mustard: Mustard seeds are a perfect fit for traditional healing magick. They absorb negative energy into themselves, storing it safely inside. After using mustard seeds in a ritual be sure to dispose of them away from your home, in order to avoid re-encountering that bad energy.

Nutmeg: Nutmeg has psychedelic properties—although I strongly advise against ingesting it. However, it can still be useful in rituals involving higher planes of existence. Communicating with beings on a higher vibrational level can be enhanced with nutmeg.

Oak: Oak trees live long lives, and because of this, they are very wise. That's why they are symbols of intuition and knowledge. Their wisdom is not something you learn from books—it's wisdom that can only be learned by listening to the trees.

Oregano: Turn to oregano if you're looking for focus and mental clarity. Burning oregano before a ritual can help center your thoughts and solidify your intention.

Pepper: Peppers are good for rituals that involve generating large amounts of spiritual energy—this could be anything from invocations to chanting mantras. All varieties will enhance your efforts, but the spicier the better. Just be sure to take precautions when handling them!

Rose: These flowers may be associated with love, but really, they represent passion of any kind. Roses are a friend of the ambitious and the dreamers. White roses in particular have associations with the Triple Goddess.

Rosemary: Rosemary is the herb to use when dealing with difficult people. It fosters empathy and goodwill. It's also a good fragrance to incorporate into meditation and creative visualization.

Saffron: This bright red, costly herb holds all sorts of mystical value. Saffron is useful for lucid dreaming, astral projection, and past life regression. It can also be used in the blessing of a home or in fertility rites.

Sage: Sage is the classic herb used for cleansing and blessing. Burning sage inside a home wards off evil spirits and protects occupants from negative energies. Sleeping with sage under your mattress or pillow can also prevent nightmares.

Thyme: Turn to thyme for practical wisdom and making tough decisions. It can provide you the clarity of mind you need to see a situation for what it really is. Thyme is also a good choice for rituals to mend a broken heart.

Tulip: No matter the hue, tulips are good for happiness and positive energy. If you're looking for a fresh start and want to commemorate it with a ritual, be sure to include tulips. Additionally, bring a bouquet of tulips to your next housewarming party. It makes a beautiful gift for the recipient and will draw positive energy into their new home.

CHAPTER 7: NATURE-BASED DEITIES

Although cultures around the world have developed their own unique pantheons of Gods and Goddesses, you almost always see at least one deity associated with the earth or nature. The natural world is of supreme importance, and nearly every spiritual tradition on earth has grasped that importance.

The Gods and Goddesses in this chapter are all associated with nature in some way or another. I'll give you a little backstory on each one, as well as some tips for incorporating them into your magickal practice.

If you are an experienced witch, you may have a particular pantheon of deities that you work with already. However, if you're an eclectic witch or haven't found the right pantheon yet, this could be the opportunity to adopt the deities of green witchcraft. These Gods and Goddesses may come from disparate traditions, but they are all unified by their close ties to the earth.

Gaia

Gaia is our wise earth mother. She brings forth and sustains life and has done so for millions of years. This Goddess is of the utmost importance in green witchcraft, and you'll find that I refer to her often in my rituals. Aside from the Triple Goddess, Gaia is the most archetypical depiction of the Divine feminine you'll find in witchcraft.

Originally from Greek mythology, Gaia is a primordial Goddess, born out of chaos. Her energy permeates the planet, and when this energy accumulates in large quantities, that place is considered holy. When witches invoke Gaia in their magick, that same holy energy is drawn into the sacred circle.

Invocations to Gaia should always be accompanied by a natural gift or offering. Fruits, vegetables, or flowers that you've grown are all good choices, as are handmade objects like a flower wreath or wood carving.

Colors associated with Gaia include white (because of her divinity) and earth tones—greens, browns, etc. This Goddess is particularly good to call on when you're looking for guidance or are unsure about the future.

Cernunnos

Cernunnos is the archetypical male God within Wicca. Sometimes referred to as the Horned God, he is the source of masculine divine energy in the natural world. Depicted as a mighty forest dweller with stag antlers, he is a symbol of living in harmony with nature. While Cernunnos is sometimes unfairly equated with the Christian Devil (because of his horns), he is a force for goodness and protection in the world.

Cernunnos oversees the yearly cycle of life, death, and rebirth. As such, he is no stranger to mourning—he's a good God to turn to when praying for the spirits of the dead.

He is at his strongest point during the winter solstice, when the earth is cold and dormant. However, there is nothing sinister about his associations with death. However, he does serve as a reminder that the natural world moves in cycles, we are part of that cycle, and one day we will reach the end of that cycle.

Ostara

Ostara is a Germanic Goddess of the spring and is another of the most important deities in witchcraft. She's so important, in fact, that she has a Wiccan holiday named after her that's celebrated at the spring equinox—the time when day and night are perfectly equal.

This Goddess is ancient, and we actually have very few writings from the earliest people who worshipped her. However, it's known that she is also a fertility Goddess and is largely responsible for the celebration of Easter. Even though her exact beginnings may have been lost to history, her worshippers continue to venerate her today.

Ostara is sometimes symbolized as a white rabbit and sometimes as a bunch of butterflies. Both of these symbols will enhance your magick when invoking her. Additionally, white, green, and pink are her colors.

Ninhursag

This ancient Sumerian Goddess is considered mother of the mountains. She's also known as the Great Lady of Heaven, and in some belief traditions, she is the principal manifestation of the Divine feminine. Ninhursag is represented by the Greek omega symbol, which has been used for much longer than the Greeks have been around. She shares this symbol with another nature-based deity, cow Goddess Hathor from Egypt.

If you're looking for a spiritual encounter in the natural world, ask Ninhursag to give you guidance and clarity. Her spirit is said to in and around the peaks of mountains, so she knows how the Divine and the physical world intermingle. Outdoor meditation sessions can always be conducted in her honor.

Geb

Geb is an Egyptian earth God who is fearsome, to say the least. Often depicted as having a viper around his head, Geb is considered the God of snakes. However, he doesn't stop there—ancient Egyptians also believed he caused earthquakes by laughing. He's definitely a God that reflects the dangerous side of nature. And that's exactly why he's important in green witchcraft.

But Geb isn't all bad. He's also responsible for making crops grow, and he was traditionally depicted as feeding his followers from vegetation grown on his own body. If you find yourself in a leadership position, turn to Geb and ask for the wisdom to use your power justly. Geb can empower us to be respected instead of feared.

CHAPTER 8: GARDENING SPELLS

Whenever possible, I highly recommend that you grow the plants and herbs you will be using in your rituals. Nurturing something from a tiny seed into a full-grown plant creates a spiritual connection between you and the earth that enhances your magick in a way that buying plants cannot. It also attunes you more closely to the cycle of the seasons—another important aspect of witchcraft.

As much as I would love to share practical gardening tips with you, that's the subject of another book! However, I do want to share with you some magickal tips and spells that will put you on the path towards a bountiful harvest.

The following are a collection of rituals, blessings, and simple folk magick tricks you can use throughout the entire growing process. With a little magick and a little luck, your garden will be in full bloom right before your eyes!

Blessing the Soil

To get your garden off to a good start, try a blessing before you begin planting. You can keep it as simple or elaborate as you want to—what's important is that you couple your blessing with a strong and genuine intention in your mind. Focus your mind on thoughts of a healthy, thriving garden—picture it as if its already a reality.

And as the growing season progresses, think back to your initial blessing from time to time.

For those that are looking for a simple, quick blessing, try this prayer to the earth:

Spirits of the soil, element of earth, bless this garden and the life that will soon spring from it. I call upon the energies of Gaia, our wise earth Mother, to bless and consecrate this ground that by the work of my hands, it will flourish and grow with life-giving plants. I set my intention and I seal my will. So mote it be.

If possible, try to schedule this prayer for the night of a full moon. This is the point of the month where positive spiritual energies are at their highest, which can help strengthen your magickal connection to the natural world. However, saying this prayer on a bright, sunny day is just as effective. The sun gives life to the plants we grow, so it's fitting to work this magick under his watchful eye.

For those that want a bit more ceremony and ritual for their blessing, the following is a longer, more involved work of magick you can use.

Items needed:
- 1 white candle
- Matches
- Bowl of water
- Bowl of apple slices
- Salt (optional)

Begin by walking the perimeter of your garden clockwise. If you would like, you can pour a ring of salt around the outside of the garden, but this is not absolutely necessary. The point of circling the garden is to create a seal that will prevent negative energies from entering—the salt merely reinforces this point in a visual way. As you walk the perimeter, repeat the prayer from earlier:

Spirits of the soil, element of earth, bless this garden and the life that will soon spring from it. I call upon the energies of Gaia, our wise earth Mother, to bless and consecrate this ground that by the work of my hands, it will flourish and grow with life-giving plants. I set my intention and I seal my will. So mote it be.

Now, take your white candle and light it. Walk to the northern edge of your garden. If it's not perfectly aligned with the cardinal directions, no worries—simply go to the side that's facing closest to north. Hold the candle above your head and say:

Spirits of the north, merry meet. I call upon your power to nourish this land. Join me as the magick unfolds.

Walk to the south and say:

Spirits of the south, merry meet. I call upon your power to consecrate this land. Join me as the magick unfolds.

Now to the west:

Spirits of the west, merry meet. I call upon your power to sustain this land. Join me as the magick unfolds.

Finally, come to the east and say:

Spirits of the east, merry meet. I call upon your power to seal this land. Join me as the magick unfolds.

Now, walk to the center of the garden. Carefully place the candle at your feet and lift your hands above your head while you repeat the following:

Welcome to all the spirits, sprites, elementals, and beings that gather here now. Welcome to the Meeting Place. May our energies work as one, may our voices be as one. May the great Goddess of the earth, our wise Mother, smile upon us and bless this place. So mote it be.

Leave the candle burning in the center of the garden (take any necessary safety precautions) and return to the edge. Take the bowl of water to the northern side and begin to sprinkle water with your fingers along the perimeter as you walk along clockwise. While you do that, repeat this short blessing:

Life-giving water, bless and replenish this ground. Quench it physically and protect it spiritually.

When you've made a full circle, place the bowl of water back on the ground and pick up the apple slices. Return to the center of the garden and hold it above your head. As you do this, say this prayer to the Goddess Gaia:

Mother Goddess, great Gaia, I invoke you in this place. May this gift of fruit grant me favor in your eyes. I call upon your natural powers and elemental energies to cleanse and bless this garden. By the work of my hand and your spirit, let all that grows within it prosper. Let the ground spring forth with your Divine beauty. So mote it be.

Take the apple slices and place them in the southeast corner of the garden. Return to the candle in the center of the garden and pick it up. As you raise it above your head, say the following:

The work is done, may we all depart in peace. May the magick linger long after we are gone. May all within this circle find their way safely home.

Now, return to the northern edge of the garden and begin to walk the perimeter counterclockwise. While you do that, say this:

The circle opens but the power remains. I seal this ground with Divine protection. Let all within its bounds prosper.

Extinguish your candle to finish the blessing ritual.

Allow the apples to remain in the garden for 24 hours. After that time has passed, bury them in the ground. This ritual should be repeated before every growing season.

Fence Post Ribbons

For a little splash of color magick, consider tying ribbons to your garden fence posts, if you've got them. You've got quite a few options when it comes to choosing particular colors. Green represents life and vitality and will encourage the healthy growth of plants. Bright yellow or white will draw in positive natural energies from nearby. Black, thanks to its magnificent banishing power, will ensure that negative energies are not allowed to infiltrate the garden.

Really, as long as you choose a color that evokes positivity from you, you'll see the benefits of this simple, magickal decoration.

Charging Your Seeds

Place your seed packets outdoors during the full moon closest to planting time. This will charge them with the spiritual energy that our lunar friend provides. This is also a great option for other gardening accessories—like tools, gardening clothes, etc. The light of the moon imbues everything it touches with divine, feminine energy, which will work in tandem with the divine, feminine energy of Mother Earth.

Fairy Mirror

According to traditional folklore, fairies, elves, imps, and other tricky magickal creatures can wreak havoc on a garden. They're highly mischievous and love irking humans with a little good-natured villainy. However, you can foil their plans by placing a small mirror at the foot of your garden gate.

Mirrors are man-made inventions and these nature-based creatures are highly fascinated with this human "magick." They'll spend all night enchanted by its reflective gaze and forget what they came to do. Then when the sun rises, it's back to their homes and hiding spots for them.

Do fairies and other creatures like that really exist? I can't say for sure, but every spring, my trusty mirror takes its rightful place at the foot of my garden gate...just in case!

Harvest Thanksgiving Ritual

When the growing season has wound down and you've harvested your last crop, take a moment to thank the earth for what it's given you. I recommend taking something you've grown and burying it back in the garden—as a token of your appreciation for all the things that you've grown.

Along with the offering, say this short prayer before you call it quits for the year:

Mother Gaia, the harvest is over and the fields grow quiet. But your life-giving power remains and waits for the next season. Please accept my offering and my gratitude for what the earth has brought forth. May we soon meet again and continue the cycle of life. Blessed be.

CHAPTER 9: SACHETS

S achets just might be my absolute favorite type of plant magick out there! Spiritually, they are incredibly potent, but they also smell wonderful and you can do lots of creative, decorative things with them too!

At its most basic, a sachet is a collection of fragrant materials (herbs, flowers, etc.) placed in a small decorative bag. Normally, they are placed in particular rooms of a home, but they're small enough that tossing one in your purse or bag is an option too—that way you can carry around its power with you!

When you plan the contents of a sachet with correspondences in mind, you can create a concoction with real magickal potency! In this chapter, I'm going to show you two basic types of sachets—banishing and attracting.

Like the name implies, a banishing sachet is one filled with herbs meant to repel negativity and bad energy. On the other hand, attracting sachets help draw positive, Divine energy into your surroundings.

Banishing Sachet

To be sufficiently powerful, your banishing sachet will need to be filled to the brim with potent herbs and flowers imbued with spiritual protection. I suggest the following combination:

- Cedar chips
- Mustard seeds
- Mint sprigs

- Goldenrod
- Rosemary
- Sage

The exact quantities can vary depending on availability and personal preference—don't be afraid to tweak your concoction based on the fragrances you like. If your nose would prefer the soft perfume of rosemary over the dominating scent of cedar then go crazy with the rosemary! All of these herbs and flowers are going to be beneficial and protective, no matter their exact configuration.

Attracting Sachet

The plants I suggest for the attracting sachet all have the positivity and Divine influence needed draw in spiritual energy from the natural world. They are powerful yet comforting, strong yet gentle. My herbal combination looks like this:

- Dried rose petals
- Lavender
- Ginger root
- Oregano leaves
- Mint (you can never have enough good luck!)

As with the banishing sachet, feel free to tweak this list according to your personal preferences. And as you become more adept at plant magick, don't be afraid to branch out and try your own completely original concoction!

Sachet Blessing Ritual

Before you assemble your sachet, take some time to bless the items being used and solidify your intention behind it. The following is a short consecration ritual meant to purify your sachet with the Divine energy of the earth.

Items Needed:

- 1 White candle
- Matches
- Sachet filling
- Sachet bag (you can find these at most craft supply stores—don't be afraid to get creative!)
- Bowl of water
- Handful of salt

Begin by clearing a space and placing all your items in one central area. Pick up the bowl of water and sprinkle the salt into it. As you do this, say:

Earth and spirit meet in salt—may it cleanse this water and fill it with the Divine energy of our Earth Mother.

Now, walk a circle clockwise around your collected items that's large enough for both them and you. As you walk, sprinkle water on the floor. While you do that, repeat the following:

This circle is sealed with the power of the spirit realm. Elementals of the earth, send your protection.

Return to your items and light the white candle. Then, recite this invocation:

Gaia, Goddess of the earth, hear my prayer. May your warmth and radiance fill this circle from the pure flame before me. Bless these tools that work my will. Charge them with the ancient energy of the ground from which they came.

If you're creating a banishing sachet, continue with this:

May my sachet protect me from evil and malevolent spirits. With your watchful eye, no evil can invade my spirit. So mote it be.

If you're creating an attracting sachet, say this instead:

May my sachet draw the life and vitality of the universe into myself. May I be a beacon of positive energy. So mote it be.

Now, take your bowl of water and lightly sprinkle each of your sachet items. You can bless the herbs individually or as a whole. Don't forget to bless the sachet bag too! As you perform this, say the following:

I seal this object with the power of the Divine Spirit. May my will be made manifest.

Once everything has been blessed, assemble your sachet there in the sacred circle. When it's complete, hold it above your head and over the flame of the candle. While you do that, say this:

The work is done and the power is manifest. May this sachet bless and protect all people and places within its range. The spell is cast and the magick begun.

Extinguish your candle and walk around your circle—but this time clockwise. As you travel, repeat the following:

Mother Gaia and all spirits of the earth gathered here, I thank you for your presence and I send you on your way. May we meet again in this happy circle someday soon. Blessed be.

Now that the ritual is done, place your sachet somewhere in your house. The foyer is a good place for banishing sachets and the living room a good place for attracting ones. However, it's really up to you. And don't forget—you can also take the sachet with you, so its power will always be nearby!

Your sachet will eventually lose some of its potency, so repeat this blessing ritual with a new one every two or three months.

CHAPTER 10: SMUDGING

Smudging is a practice that began in Native American cultures, but over time other groups have adopted it as well—it's particularly popular in many types of witchcraft. While the specific materials and techniques may vary from culture to culture, at its core, smudging is a plant-based way to harness the magickal power of smoke.

This practice involves burning herbs, flowers, or other plants and wafting the resulting smoke throughout a room or other area. Some people smudge to banish negative energy and evil. Others use it as part of an invocation to a God or Goddess. It can also be a great way to bless a new home.

There are many reasons a green witch might want to use smudging (and I encourage you come up with your own), but no matter the reason, you're always tapping into the sacred, mystic power of smoke. You are setting someplace apart as important and sacred. The fragrance will linger longer after the ritual is done, reminding you that it's a place of intention and spiritual energy.

In this chapter, we'll be looking at the different methods of smudging you can use, as well as what herbs are good for this practice. Then, I'll walk you through an actual smudging blessing ritual. While a formal ceremony isn't always necessary, it's yet another way that you can bring importance and symbolism into the place you're blessing.

Methods of Smudging

The most iconic method of smudging involves bundling herbs into what is known as a smudging stick. The end of this stick is lit and the user then directs the smoke by moving it around. This method is convenient because it requires no other tools besides the herbs themselves, and it allows you the freedom to direct the smoke anywhere you wish.

However, creating a smudging stick is not as simple as just grabbing a handful of herbs. There is an art to it, and if you're not experienced, I highly recommend buying one from somebody else. You're supporting a fellow seeker, and you don't have to worry about accidentally charring your fingertips!

The other popular method of smudging involves placing the herbs in a fireproof bowl (emphasis on the "fireproof") and setting them on fire. This is the method I recommend for the smudging beginner, since putting some herbs into a bowl is much easier than trying to assemble a smudging stick. If you want to move the smoke in a particular direction or send it to a particular area, wave your hand over the bowl, use your breath, or use a feather.

Herbs for Smudging

You'll want to choose smudging herbs based on what corresponds well with your intention. You can refer back to the earlier chapter of correspondences if you'd like, but I've provided some below for quick reference too.

Sage: When people think of smudging, sage is the first herb that comes to mind. It's traditionally used to cleanse an area of malevolent entities or negative energy. Pre-made smudging sticks are typically sage, so finding this herb should not be a problem.

Cedar: Like I mentioned earlier, smudging can be used during invocations as an offering or other part of the ritual. If you want to go this route, use cedar because of its associations with the Divine. Cedar trees are usually associated with masculine energy, so use it especially with male deities.

Fennel: Fennel sprigs are a good smudging option when you want to harness the energies of the earth. They are closely associated with elemental magick and the physical world in general. Try burning fennel in your home if you live in the city but want to stay connected to nature.

Lavender: Lavender smoke perfumes the air with psychic energy and spiritual insight. It can be quite beneficial to burn some lavender before performing a tarot card reading, a séance, or other paranormal art. It can also foster lucid dreaming, so burn some in your bedroom if you're looking to master that skill.

Basil: When in doubt, use basil. It's a great herb for drawing in positive general energy for a wide number of purposes. If you're not sure what you want to smudge for, basil is a safe choice that will allow you to see what all the fuss is about. It invigorates a space with good vibes and good luck.

Smudging Ritual

The following is a simple smudging ritual you can use at home. It's not particularly long or complex, but it will allow you the opportunity to focus clearly and single-mindedly on your intention. It's written for use with the bowl method or the smudging stick method.

Items Needed:
- Fireproof bowl or smudging stick
- Loose herbs (if using bowl)
- Matches

Enter the room you want to bless and stand in the center. Bow to the west and say the following:

Spirits of the west wind, send goodwill my way. Let your mighty gusts permeate and consecrate this place.

Now light the herbs in your bowl or light the end of your smudging stick. Be patient—give it just a bit of time to get smoking steadily. Relight the herbs as necessary.

Beginning at the northernmost point of the room, walk its perimeter clockwise. As you do, repeat your intention as succinctly as possible, beginning with, "This place is..." For example, you might say:

This place is sealed with spiritual protection.

The exact words you choose will depend on the personal purpose of this smudging ceremony.

As you walk, try to waft the smoke all over the place. You can also move the bowl or smudging stick up and down, left and right in front of you. If you'd like to create a ritualized movement to use, that's fine, but you can also just wing it.

At this point, you might want to walk a ceremonial path through the room, if you have the desire and the space. If you're looking for ideas, consider walking the path of a five-pointed star laid out on the floor. Or you could walk the outline of the symbol of the Triple Goddess. Get creative and find a shape or a path that's meaningful to you.

When you're done with the smudging ritual, be extra sure that your herbs are completely extinguished. Use the same caution and care as you would with any burning object. Once you're certain that everything is out, dispose of the ashes outdoors—allow them to blow away in the wind, if possible. If you were using a smudging stick and there are still herbs left, wrap the stick in a special cloth (treat it with the respect it deserves) and store it away for safekeeping.

By Didi Clarke

CHAPTER 11: TINCTURES

Tinctures take time and patience—from start to finish, the process lasts about a month. But, in exchange for all that waiting, you're left with an herbal concoction that can be used for all sorts of magickal applications.

A tincture is simply a mixture of herbs and alcohol, and they've been used for centuries by witches and non-witches alike. The herbs are allowed to steep for a month or more, infusing the liquid with their fragrance and spiritual power. Then, they're strained away, and you're left with the concentrated essence of that herb in tincture form.

Within green witchcraft, tinctures are commonly used as a form of blessing or protecting—they're similar in purpose to anointing oil. Objects or people (more on that in a minute) anointed with a tincture are sealed with the natural energies of the particular herb that was used.

Before we go any further, a word of caution—under no circumstances should you drink or otherwise ingest a tincture. Additionally, use caution if you're going to apply one to yourself or someone else topically. Just because you're a witch doesn't mean you're magickally immune to allergies or irritants. Some of these herbs can be very potent when in concentrated form. And if you do apply one topically, you only need a small amount to experience its power.

In the following sections, I'll recommend some herbs for creating tinctures, and I'll show you how to bless and assemble the actual tincture itself. You'll be opening up your own apothecary before you know it!

Herbs for Tinctures

Like in the previous chapters, I highly recommend that you return to the correspondence section of this book to find the perfect herb (or herbs) for your particular purposes. Below, I've shared a few of my favorite combinations and what they're good for.

When making a tincture, always be sure to use fresh herbs, not dried ones. And don't skimp on them, add as many as the size of your container will allow.

Lavender and Honeysuckle: I know you're probably sick of lavender by this point, but I can't get enough of it. This combo is great for blessing a bedroom. The lavender will encourage sweet dreams, and the honeysuckle is an all-purpose attractor of positive energy. Try placing a small amount of the tincture on your bed frame or above the door.

Rose Petals: While it's not like in the movies, love potions are indeed a real part of witchcraft. And a fragrant rose petal tincture is just what you need to stoke the flames of romance! Dab a little bit of this on your wrists before a big date for confidence and charm. Or try it when you want to feel sexy for that special someone!

Lilies: Lily blossoms represent purity, so they're a perfect choice if you're looking for a tincture that can be used for blessings. From anointing the hearth of a new home to christening a new car, use a lily tincture major milestones and new beginnings.

Tincture Assembly and Blessing

The following is a short blessing ritual you can perform over your herbs and tincture container. I recommend a small mason jar, but any kind of glass bottle that seals tightly (you'll be shaking it from time to time) should work. Ribbons or other jar ornamentations are highly encouraged!

After that, I'll show you how to assemble the ingredients and how to nurture your tincture to fruition!

Items Needed:

- High-proof alcohol (rubbing alcohol or vinegar can be used instead)
- Glass container
- Herbs (enough to fill the container)
- Cheesecloth (for later in the process)

To bless your items, take them outside on a sunny day. One at a time, hold them in your hands and raise them towards the sun. As you do, say this:

I bless this object with the Divine radiance of the sun. It is filled with power and potential.

When you've blessed each object individually, hold your hands over all of them and say:

May all the parts work in unity to achieve my singular will. They are blessed and sealed with harmony, prosperity, and warmth from the life-giving sun.

Once this short blessing is completed, it's time to assemble your tincture. Begin by placing all your herbs into the glass jar. As I mentioned earlier, pack as many in there as will fit—but be sure to leave a small amount of space at the top.

Next, pour your alcohol in. Once again, leave a small space at the top of the jar.

Finally, seal the jar tightly and allow the jar to sit in a cool, dry place for at least four weeks. If you can manage to wait longer, go for it—the longer the herbs steep, the more powerful the concoction will be. Every day or two, give the jar a good shake to ensure that the essence of the herbs is distributed evenly.

You shouldn't allow your tincture to sit in direct sunlight—as the heat can alter and degrade the chemical structure of the plants. However, I highly recommend you allow your tincture to sit overnight under at least one full moon. The objects have already been blessed by the sun, so it only makes sense to bless them with the Divine power of the moon as well.

When you can't wait anymore, re-open your jar and use the cheesecloth to strain the liquid from the herbal dregs. They should be disposed of outside, if possible. Now you're left with a full-fledged tincture!

Pour it back into the glass jar and return it to its cool, dry place.

CHAPTER 12: EVERYDAY PLANT MAGICK

N ow, I am a big fan of ritual magick. I love planning out what to say and do, and there's no feeling like stumbling upon the perfect correspondence for a spell. However, plant magick doesn't always have to be formal. Its origins can be traced back to rural folk magick traditions (especially in Europe), which means that there is a long history of witches weaving the practice into their lives in mundane, everyday ways.

So, in this chapter, I'm going to show you some simpler, everyday ways to incorporate green witchcraft into your life. And it should come as no surprise that many of these traditions center around the kitchen—it's the one place in the home where there's no shortage of herbs and other tasty plants!

Decorating Potted Plants

If you're growing plants in pots to use for magickal purposes, don't be afraid to get creative and give them a little decoration! It might not make your plants grow to full size overnight, but ornamentation can lend subtle positive energies that will encourage happy, healthy plants.

For starters, I like to draw sigils, runes, or other symbols on all my pots. The pentacle (or five-pointed star) is an old favorite, but don't be afraid to incorporate other symbols that are meaningful to you. The sign of the Triple Goddess or a trinity knot are two other great options to start with, if you're looking for ideas.

Certain colors of ribbon can also bring in positive spiritual energy. Green is the obvious choice, as it represents life and vegetation, but white (representing Divinity) is another potent option. Other color choices include yellow (luck/the sun), red (passion), and orange (resilience and strength).

Head of Garlic on the Window Sill

I'm not sure where this tradition came from, but when I was a child, my mother always had a full head of garlic placed on the window sill in front of the kitchen sink. She said it was for good luck and culinary skill.

Although I'm not sure about garlic's ability to make you a better cook, it absolutely has protective spiritual qualities that make it good to keep around the kitchen. It banishes any negative energy in its presence and can help improve a person's mood as well. And believe me, you definitely want folks in a good mood if they're about to dig in to one of your dishes!

Additionally, placing a line of salt along a kitchen window sill can help protect the space from negative energy and bad spirits.

Nail in a Fruit Tree

This unusual yet popular tradition comes from old time farmers in the Appalachian Mountains—and some people absolutely swear by it. It's deceptively simple. All you do is hammer a rusty nail (and it's got to be rusty) into the trunk of a fruit tree to ensure a big harvest from it.

If I'm being honest, I'm not entirely sure what this is supposed to do or symbolize exactly, but like I said, it's wildly popular among farmers—so it must have some sort of real benefit!

Yams for Newlyweds

If you know of a young couple that will be tying the knot soon, consider giving them yams as a wedding present. Yep, you heard me right—yams.

These tasty root vegetables are traditionally associated with fertility and sensuality, which are two things that anyone beginning a new family needs some of! Whether they're eaten or simply displayed, yams can work their magick in any form.

Never Store Potatoes and Onions Together

This tradition has its roots in practical wisdom—the gases that onions release can cause potatoes to grow eyes and spoil faster than normal. However, combining these two is also seen as bad luck.

Onions are great for sucking the negative energy out of a room—they absorb all that badness into themselves, where it can be safely disposed of. But when paired with potatoes, which are traditionally used to amplifying the energies of a room, they can actual help negative energy grow and thrive.

Basil for a Good Deal

For most of us, dealing with a salesman or being in a situation where we're expected to bargain and haggle is a stressful scenario. However, next time you're off to the auction or the flea market, bring along a basil leaf to put in your pocket.

It's traditionally associated with money and prosperity, and invoking its power will help give you the spiritual upper hand in any negotiation. Use it when your wallet is full and you want it to stay that way! A simple rub of the leaf is all that you need.

Planting Based on the Day of the Week

Choose the day you decide to plant carefully—they each have different correspondences and energies associated with them. Here's a short look at which each day of the week is best for.

Sunday: Plant flowers and other delicate plants on a Sunday. It will energize them spiritually and make them more resilient.

Monday: Mondays are good for root vegetables like carrots, radishes, and potatoes.

Tuesday: If you're a little behind schedule with your planting, aim for a Tuesday. It will give your plants the extra boost of luck they need to catch up.

Wednesday: Plant herbs that will be used for divination on a Wednesday. The day's association with the Divine will imbue them with spiritual wisdom and Divine consciousness.

Thursday: Peppers and tangy fruits should be planted on a Thursday. It's a day full of energy and vibrancy, and planting them then will ensure they grow with a maximum kick.

Friday: Friday is a day of vivid color and enthusiasm, so plant bright, colorful fruits and vegetables then. Blueberries, tulips, heirloom tomatoes and other eye-catching foods are all great options for Fridays.

Saturday: If possible, avoid planting on Saturdays altogether. It is associated with the dead and with winter.

CHAPTER 13: SEASONAL MAGICK

The changing of the seasons is incredibly important in the natural world, and so it's obviously important in the practice of plant magick as well. The seasons and the weather they bring dictate the growth cycle of everything living on the planet. We track this cyclical movement not only to ensure a healthy harvest but also to honor and commemorate the natural rhythms of our earth.

While there are many points in this seasonal process witches choose to celebrate, the four big ones are the spring and fall equinoxes, as well as the summer and winter solstices.

The equnioxes mark the two points in the year when daytime and nighttime are perfectly equal—with the days getting longer after the spring equinox and the nights doing the same after the fall one. On the other hand, the solstices mark the points on the calendar when either day or night is at their longest—day in the summer and night in the winter.

In this chapter, I'll be showing you some ideas for your own seasonal celebrations. Like I mentioned, these four days are some of the most important in all of witchcraft (not just green witchcraft), so it's important to give them a heartfelt effort!

Spring Equinox

While the exact times vary from crop to crop, the spring equinox traditionally marks the beginning of the growing season. At this point in time, the earth is slowly returning to life after the cold of winter, and so the spring equinox marks a time of renewal and new beginnings.

As I talked about in the nature-based deity chapter, some witches choose to commemorate the goddess Ostara during the spring equinox because of her depiction as a young woman of child-bearing age—both iconic symbols of the life and growth that come with the spring.

If you use an altar for your spellwork, be sure to deck it out with all sorts of bright flowers and other plants during the spring equinox—and don't be afraid to pin a rose or other blossom to your shirt too! Additionally, plant offerings to Gods and Goddesses associated with the springtime are perfect for the equinox as well.

The colors associated with the spring equinox include green, pink, white, yellow, and light blue. But really, any of the bright, sunny pastels we normally associate with the springtime are appropriate in rituals and celebrations.

If you're new to the world of witchcraft, this is also a great time of year to start your magickal journey officially. Setting an intention of new study and practice fit in perfectly with the themes of the spring equinox.

Summer Solstice

The sun is at the height of its power during the summer solstice. From this point forward, the days will begin to get shorter—but for this one glorious time of year, the daylight reigns supreme.

You might hear some witches refer to this time as midsummer or Litha, but no matter what you call it, it's one of the most important days of the magickal year. Traditionally, witches have honored sun deities during the solstice or performed rituals involving the sun. However, this is also a good time of year for any magick that focuses on passion and power—two attributes we closely link to the sun.

Reds, yellows, oranges, and golds are all common colors you'll see in summer solstice celebrations, but feel free to use any hue that makes you feel empowered and energized.

Fall Equinox

The fall equinox marks the end of the harvest and the beginning of our descent into the cold, dark stillness of winter. However, this isn't a time for despair or dreariness! It's a time to honor the inevitable turn of the seasons and learn to accept them with grace.

Because of this, the fall equinox is a time to focus on balance and harmony. It is a time for remembering that we're all a part of this moving and ever-changing cycle. Many witches also use this time of the year for honoring the deceased—although this is a popular theme for the winter solstice as well.

The colors of the fall equinox include earth tones (brown, dark red, and dark green particularly), gold, silver, and black. These represent prosperity but also hint at the darkness of the season yet to come.

Winter Solstice

At the winter solstice, the world is cold and quiet. Long, sunny days have finally given way to the chilly night, and the earth is at rest. This is the day that marks the beginning of the rebirth of the sun, so in a way, it is a time of anticipation and joy.

However, it is also a great time for banishment and protection. If you're looking to break a bad habit, the winter solstice is the point of the year when your efforts will be most successful. Additionally, blessing and sealing a home or garden are also activities that work well with the solstice.

Traditional colors associated with the solstice include black, white, brown, gray, and red.

CHAPTER 14: EMBRACE THE MAGICK OF THE NATURAL WORLD

B y now, we've hit all the major things you need to know to get started with plant magick. And hopefully, even if you don't remember every little thing I've gone over, it's my sincere desire that you've come to have a deeper appreciation of the natural world and the spiritual power that it's capable of.

Green witchcraft is not an art for the impatient. Magick works on its own timetable, and this is especially true of green magick—where we must also abide by the clock that Mother Nature sets for growth and harvest. However, if you're willing to take the plunge, plant magick will put you in touch with the Divine in a way that only nature can. It teaches you to recognize the spark of magick in mundane, everyday things—like the fruits and vegetables we enjoy on a daily basis.

Whether you're looking to become a full-blown witchy farmer or a simple herbal enthusiast, it's my hope that what I've written has been instructive and transformative—just like the lessons that the earth teaches us day by day, season by season, and year by year.

If you enjoyed what you read, please consider signing up for my email list. You'll be notified every time I publish a new book or have something exciting in the works. When you sign up, you'll also receive a free color magick correspondence chart that's perfect for enhancing your spellwork spiritually and visually! Use the following link to find the sign-up page: https://mailchi.mp/01863952b9ff/didi-clarke-mailing-list

Additionally, I would be extremely grateful for an honest review of the book. I want to provide my readers with spells and magickal rituals that are important and useful to them, and receiving your feedback is one way I can better serve you.

Blessed Be,

Didi

CHAPTER 15: READ MORE FROM DIDI CLARKE

Forbidden Wiccan Spells: Magick for Love and Power (Vol. 1)

Enchant your way to romance with these Wiccan love spells! Become a master of power magick! Learn all this and much more with this original spell book from Didi Clarke!

Whether you're trying to seduce that special someone or want to show others who's the boss, *Forbidden Wiccan Spells: Magick for Love and Power* has something for everyone. With each chapter, you'll find authentic Wiccan magic that will help you unlock your dreams in love and life!

What You'll Find

Within the pages of *Magick for Love and Power*, you'll find one-of-a-kind spells written and tested by Didi Clarke herself—you won't find books on witchcraft like this anywhere else!

If you're new to Wicca, never fear—this book uses a wicca for beginners approach. The spells are explained thoroughly, and each one comes with a detailed item list and step-by-step directions.

And there's plenty for more experienced witches too. These unique magick rituals will enhance your skills and help you tap into the full potential of love and power! In this book, you'll find a wide variety of magickal practices to explore, including:

- Herbal Magick
- Candle Magick
- Mantra Magick
- Elemental Magick

Are you ready to spice up your life with love spells?

Love is a powerful force, and when you combine it with the power of witchcraft, the results can be truly magickal! In *Magick for Love and Power*, you'll get access to genuine spells and rituals that will help you attract romance into your life and keep the flames of love burning for years to come!

These love spells include:

- Flame gazing to find your true love
- Mantras to keep your partner faithful
- Potions to repair a damaged relationship
- And much more!

Are you ready to harness the strength of power magick?

These power spells are here to change your life for the better. Whether you want to be more assertive at work or tap into the power of the Spirits, this magick will leave you feeling confident and strong!

Here are some of the power spells you'll find in this complete book of witchcraft:

- Amulets for persuasive power
- Rituals for fame
- Incantations for dominance
- Many more!

Learn the Art of Love Magick and Power Magick Today!

Unlock the secrets of witchcraft within the pages of this Wiccan book of shadows written for those seeking love and power! If you're ready to take control and live your best life, read *Magick for Love and Power* today!

Forbidden Wiccan Spells: Magick for Wealth and Prosperity (Vol. 2)

Find true prosperity with these original money spells from Didi Clarke!

Are you ready to embrace the bounty of the Spirit world? Then this is the book for you! *Forbidden Wiccan Spells: Magick for Wealth and Prosperity* lays out everything you need to know in order to master the art of prosperity magick.

What You'll Find

Within the pages of *FWS: Magick for Wealth and Prosperity*, you'll find never-before-seen money spells that will help put you on the right track for financial success. From herbal magick to incantations, the rituals in this book teach you a wide variety of Wiccan magick—it's perfect for everyone from the complete beginner to the seasoned witch!

These spells include:

- A fire incantation for financial windfall
- An herbal sachet for business success
- Mantras for material prosperity
- Crystal blessings for attracting wealthy people
- And much more!

Are You Ready to Transform Your Life With Money Magick?

These spells won't make you a millionaire overnight—nothing can do that—but that doesn't mean you can't seek help from the Spirit world for money matters! This misunderstood but incredibly effective branch of magick has helped countless witches, Wiccans, and other spiritually minded people take charge of their finances in amazing ways.

Explore These Powerful Spells Today!

Each of these rituals has been written and tested by Didi Clarke herself. They're presented in an easy-to-read, step-by-step format and include a detailed item list and suggestions for achieving maximum potency. What are you waiting for? Embrace the wealth of the Universe today with *FWS: Magick for Wealth and Prosperity*!

Forbidden Wiccan Spells: Dark Goddess Magick (Vol. 3)

Darkness isn't a place of evil—it's a creative force for good that empowers Wiccans and Witches just like you! If you want to learn never-before-seen invocations, spells, and rituals that honor powerful Goddesses, this is the book for you!

Forbidden Wiccan Spells: Dark Goddess Magick explores the many Goddesses associated with darkness—Goddesses of the moon, of sleep, of dreams, and yes, even of death. For too long, those afraid of divine feminine power have told us that these Goddesses are "demons" or "monsters" or practitioners of "black magick." But Didi Clarke is here to set the record straight. These divine beings are powerful allies for any witch that approaches them with a clean heart and pure will.

Within the pages of *FWS: Dark Goddess Magick*, you'll find twelve completely original invocations that have been written and performed by Didi herself. In addition to popular Goddesses like Hecate (Goddess of the dead) and Freyja (Goddess of war), you'll find rituals involving lesser-known dark Goddesses like:

- Breksta (Goddess of dreams)
- Oya (Goddess of storms)
- Selene (Goddess of the moon)
- And many more!

Each chapter provides an easy-to-understand history of a particular Goddess, as well as correspondences associated with her. Next, you'll find an item list and step-by-step instructions for a ritual invoking one of these powerful beings. These rituals touch on many different elements of the Craft and include:

- Protection of your home
- Prophetic dreams
- Developing magickal abilities
- Communing with the dead
- Wiccan candle magick
- Wiccan herb magick
- Wiccan crystal magick
- Much more!

Whether you're looking for a book about Wicca for beginners or are a seasoned witch, whether you're a solitary witch or work with a coven, FWS: Dark Goddess Magick has something for you. It's a great addition to your spell book or your book of shadows! Embrace the power of the dark Goddess within and read it today!

Forbidden Wiccan Spells: Tarot Cards and Psychic Development Rituals (Vol. 4)

Are you ready to master the skills it takes to become a world-class tarot card reader? Are you looking for proven rituals and techniques that will enhance your psychic development?

Forbidden Wiccan Spells: Tarot Cards and Psychic Development Rituals has the answers you're looking for!

Psychic development and the art divination are two of the most misunderstood Spiritual practices out there. But despite the stereotypes, these tools are used every day by rational, ordinary people trying to make better decisions and improve their lives.

In this book, Didi Clarke provides you with everything you need to start transforming your own life with the wisdom of the psychic realm!

What You'll Find

Within the pages of *FWS: Tarot Cards and Psychic Development Rituals*, you'll find a comprehensive breakdown of everything you need to become a confident, insightful tarot card reader. From card meanings to developing your own reading style, this book is perfect for beginners or experienced readers who want a refresher course.

In addition to this tarot handbook, you'll also find completely original spells and rituals meant to enhance your psychic abilities. Whether you want to get better at dream interpretation, reading tea leaves, or anything between, these magickal rituals will help you harness the power of the Spirit world to reach that goal!

Unlock The Future With Tarot Card Readings

Tarot cards are by far one of the most popular forms of divination available. Unfortunately, becoming a proficient reader can seem like an uphill battle—but it doesn't have to be like that!

Within the pages of *FWS: Tarot Cards and Psychic Development Rituals*, Didi Clarke addresses the most important things every tarot card reader needs to know, including:

- Card meanings for all 78 cards
- Major themes of the four minor arcana suits
- Choosing the right card spread
- Memorizing meanings vs. intuitive reading
- Identifying relationships and themes across cards

Hone Your Divination Skills With Psychic Development

Tarot is a fantastic tool, but there is so much more to explore in the world of divination too!

If you're ready to expand your psychic abilities in more ways than one, these spells and rituals should leave you feeling insightful and powerful. The rituals include:

- Invoking Gods of prophecy
- Herbal magick to aid dream interpretation
- Automatic writing
- Meditation for encountering spirit guides
- Candle magick for finding lost objects

Don't forget to sign up for my mailing list and receive your free color magick correspondence chart by following the link below!

https://mailchi.mp/01863952b9ff/didi-clarke-mailing-list

Manufactured by Amazon.ca
Bolton, ON

10962477R00039